D1120205

Fifty Years at the
GRAND OLE OPRY

Other Books by Myron Tassin

THE LAST LINE: A Streetcar Named St. Charles (1973)
THE DELTA QUEEN: Last of the Paddlewheel Palaces (1974)
BACCHUS (1975)

Fifty Years at the "GRAND OLE OPRY

By
MYRON TASSIN
and
JERRY HENDERSON

Foreword by
MINNIE PEARL

Introduction by
MOTHER MAYBELLE CARTER

PELICAN PUBLISHING COMPANY

GRETNA 1975

Library of Congress Cataloging in Publication Data

Tassin, Myron.
    Fifty years at the Grand Ole Opry.
    SUMMARY: A pictorial history of the Grand Ole Opry,
the Nashville radio program that is a "symbol of country
music to the world."
    1. Grand Ole Opry (Radio Program).   2. Country
music—United States—Juvenile Literature. [1. Grand
Ole Opry (Radio Program) 2. Country Music]   I. Henderson, Jerry, joint author. II. Title.
ML3930.G72T35   791.44'7   75–15846
ISBN 0-88289-089-1

Designed by Barney McKee
Manufactured in the United States of America
Published by Pelican Publishing Company, Inc.
630 Burmaster Street, Gretna, Louisiana   70053

Contents

*Minnie Pearl and Roy Acuff on stage at the Ryman Auditorium
at the last performance before the move to Opryland.*

Dedication

WE love the Grand Ole Opry because her children are our friends. And as our friends they understand us, and appreciate our desires to adhere unashamedly to our own particular way of life. Throughout the fifty years of the Opry's existence, her performers have been gifted in always making us feel at home—but two of them have been exceptional in this. It is because both these entertainers can carry us back to the mountain so easily . . . to the pleasant country scenes as well as to the almost sacred remembrances of hardships and sorrows . . . back to the innocent and sincere people whose uncles, cousins and brothers make that life dear to us . . . and because, through being innovators in their own areas, they represent the Grand Ole Lady as two of her most prominent children, we fondly dedicate this book to Roy Acuff and Minnie Pearl.

Foreword

HOWDEEE!

The Grand Ole Opry and country music have been a part of my life for thirty some odd years (and some have been pretty odd, I'll tell you!). I love the sound, the participation of performer and listener, the shared joy, and the camaraderie that exists among all who work in the country music field. I love for folks to write about it. It may interest someone who has never tried it before.

Therefore, I am happy to see a book like this go on the market. A great deal of resource and research has gone into it. Very obviously, the authors care about our music—and we appreciate that! Thank you.

Minnie Pearl

MINNIE PEARL
Nashville, Tennessee

Introduction

COUNTRY music reflects to us a way of life; it mirrors feelings, incidents, and ideals of a world that is very close and dear to many of us. Because we cherish our separateness and independent ways, our style of life might have gone unnoticed by America had it not been for our music.

When we sang, we sang of people and places that were familiar to us—neighbors, friends, the home place, and gatherings that we knew better than anyone else. When we sang, we sang of problems—hard work, poverty, sorrow—problems that were part of our everyday life. When we sang, we sang of hopes and prayers—that opportunity would come and free us from the hardships of our life or that we would have a better home waiting in the sky. And when we sang, we sang to others who knew the same people, places, and problems, and who had the same hopes and prayers.

The Grand Ole Opry sprang from such a neighborly sharing, and has become the symbol of country music to the world. She became that because she has always given, to those of us who were part of her as well as to the remainder of interested America, a down-to-earth and straightforward picture of a way of life.

To all who have ever been a part of her—either standing in the center of her stage and picking *Wildwood Flower*, or pulling the ropes to change her scenery, or announcing her name over the airways, or selling her programs to people visiting from all over America, or applauding her stars from the audience, or listening by a radio and patting a foot—to all of us, she is truly a "grand lady."

Maybelle Carter

MOTHER MAYBELLE CARTER
Nashville, Tennessee

Ernest Tubb

Fifty Years at the
GRAND OLE OPRY

CHAPTER I

A neighbor to talk to ...that's worth a lot!

"**J**UST poor folks, that's all we were, trying to make a living out of black land dirt."

We said it as hard, cold fact. Depressing, perhaps, but very realistic! We believed in being simple and straightforward in expressing our feelings and we wanted our friends to express themselves the same way. Perhaps because we felt that singing seemed to help the troubled soul, we rural southerners were fond of singing—so much so that among us singing was almost as universal as speaking. It was only natural that our music took on the characteristics of our deeply rooted attitudes.

Fred Rose of Acuff–Rose Publishing Company in Nashville has said that he never truly understood the real meaning of country music until he stood backstage at the Grand Ole Opry and watched Roy Acuff, tears streaming from his eyes, sing a tragic song about a dying child, *Don't Make Me Go to Bed and I'll Be Good.*

But is it the singer alone which makes country music so effective? What about the girl who, after the accidental death of her husband, sits in a diner and listens through tears to the Davis Sisters singing *I've Forgot More than You'll Ever Know?* Without her and other girls like her who have lost their loves to death, to other women, or to other interests, and who need someone with whom to share that heartache, the music might pass unnoticed. There is an unashamed down-to-earth sharing in country music—a communication.

It is the unsophisticated and straightforward attitude of both the singer and the listener that has made this music flourish and has given birth to the Grand Ole Lady of country music, the Grand Ole Opry. Hank Williams, one of the Opry's monuments, said it all with just one word: sincerity. "When a hillbilly sings a crazy song," Williams said, "he feels crazy." "When he sings *I Laid My Mother Away,* he sees her a-laying right there in the coffin. He sings more sincere than most entertainers because the hillbilly was raised rougher than most entertainers. You got to know a lot about hard work. You got to have smelt mule manure before you can sing like a hillbilly. The people who has been raised something like the way the hillbilly has, knows what he is singing about and appreciates it."

FIFTY YEARS AT THE GRAND OLE OPRY

From the union of such honesty and comradeship prevalent in the rural South the Grand Ole Opry was born. Through a half century the Opry has continued to grow by being a sounding board for those of us who want to sing and those millions of us who want to listen to words that tell, like it really is, about our own interests and problems.

True, our interests and problems have changed through the years as our religious, social, cultural, and economic patterns have changed, but these changes have helped us develop a stronger love for our own music and helped us spread this love to other people. The Grand Ole Lady has now firmly planted her roots all over the world, like a giant oak which is nurtured rather than shaken by the winds of progress. However, it is doubtful that such a tree could have been planted at any other time in American history. During the 1920s, '30s, and '40s, there was not only plenty of fertile land, but the seed was available, and there were plenty of sincere hard workers to plant and nourish it along to maturity.

But times have changed. In 1950 there were 7 million farmers in the United States; in the late '60s there were only 3 million . . . and of these only one million were responsible for 90 percent of the nation's output. As the small farm falls to subdivisions of asphalt and concrete, with it goes the way of life which gave birth to the Opry. Rural musical styles have been altered so much that there are few seeds available. The styles of the earlier performers were the result of deeply ingrained beliefs and feelings bred by a southern rural lifestyle which is fast fading from the American scene. Commercialism has threatened much of the neighborly flavor which was such a vital part of the Opry's planting and formative years.

The Grand Ole Opry was founded at a time when the radio was beginning to reach into areas of the United States that previously had been in relative isolation—the rural South, where people preferred music that communicated to them . . . music they could relate to. Uncle Jimmy Thompson's fiddle style was an immediate success with Nashville's wsm listeners because they saw country music as a neighborly function, where the entertainer performs for his own enjoyment and that of his friends, and anyone is welcome to join in. Other amateur musicians began to join in at wsm. These farmers and laborers provided entertainment without pay for their friends and neighbors, never realizing that they were planting a seedling which would grow into one of America's strongest institutions. The radio program was like an old-fashioned southern hoedown where the performers were simply any of the home folk who could play an instrument.

Such activities are still a part of our lives, and not only when the radio dial is tuned to 650 on Saturday nights. The scene comes to our mind of John Ramey of Linden, Tennessee, tapping his foot and fiddling vigorously while three of his neighbors join him with guitars and a banjo . . . playing for those of us who are sitting on the bed, chairs, or on the floor of the front room of his house. Surrounded by photographs on the walls of sons and nephews who had been away to war, a picture of "The Last Supper" over the mantle, and the family Bible lying on the sewing machine, such a get-together could be expected any Friday night at Mr. John's. What numbers did they play, and each from memory? . . . *Arkansas Traveler, Turkey in the Straw,* and others . . . the same fiddle tunes that were played by the Possum Hunters on the WSM Barn Dance in the 1920s.

It is such performers and listeners who cherish this neighborly feeling for each other that have made the Grand Ole Opry. As the Opry has matured, many things have changed, but the neighborly feeling has prevailed. When the Duke of Paducah said, "I'm going back to the wagon, these shoes are killin' me," we felt at home and free to loosen our shoelaces, or even take off our shoes if they cramped our feet. When Minnie Pearl shouts, "Howd-e-e, I'm just so proud to be here," when Porter Wagoner says, "It's time to go to the house, folks," and when little Jimmy Dickens sings "Y'all come," vital signs of a spirit which has made the Grand Ole Lady grand are being manifested.

Our music has always discussed life in a franker, more realistic manner than any other form of music and has usually dealt with simple, fundamental subjects—God and His actions, home and family, man's environment and friends, and such romantic problems as infidelity, divorce, and unrequited love. These have always been important subjects to rural America, and somehow, justly or otherwise, we have never actually trusted city folk to understand our problems. Even though the city has always been a temptation to rural dwellers, many never learned its true nature; and many who did found discontentment. It was only natural, therefore, that the people from the little towns and crossroads of the Appalachian states felt more at ease and relaxed when listening to singers from hometowns similar to our own—Poor Valley, Virginia; Maynardsville, Tennessee; Ironton, Ohio; Bulls Gap, Tennessee; Harman, West Virginia; Muskogee, Oklahoma; Cottonport, Louisiana; and Dry Ridge, Kentucky. The songs seemed even closer to home when we knew that the singer had been a tenant farmer, had worked in the coal mines or textile mills, had driven a logging truck, or had picked cotton or peanuts. The singers were like neighbors from "down the lane" . . . and there was nothing like good neighbors!

"This world is not my home, I'm just a passin' through," was a firm belief in that section of America which H. L. Mencken labeled the Bible Belt in the 1920s. When the question of teaching the theory of evolution in schoolrooms arose in 1925, the strong support which Tennessee and the South gave William Jennings Bryan in the famous "Monkey Trial" of Dayton, Tennessee, emphasized a firm and unquestioning belief in God. And furthermore, in a God who was always watching . . . and waiting to provide a heavenly home.

For years country music performers have encouraged their friends who are enduring hardships and sorrows, counseling that "farther along we'll understand why." The Carter Family was strongly representative of such attitudes with their spirituals *Room in Heaven for Me* and *I've Got a Home in Glory*. In addition to our farmers being taught at church and camp meetings, Opry performers also assured them that "there's a better home awaitin' in the sky"; it might be "just a cabin in the corner of glory land," but it would give them an opportunity to "just hear the angels sing and shake Jesus' hand."

The fundamentalist belief in the necessity for emotionalism in religion, which was prominent in the '20s and which has continued to some extent in the South, complemented our people's inclination to express themselves in music. In 1936, Roy Acuff, son of a Smoky Mountains tenant farmer, made his first and perhaps most significant recording, based on a biblical passage. Jeremiah 12:9 states, "Mine heritage is unto me as a great speckled bird, the birds round about are against her." Acuff made *The Great Speckled Bird* nationally famous, and it became a standard hymn in many Pentecostal Holiness Churches. It was a song of consolation, assuring listeners that they would be "joyfully carried to meet Him on the wings of that great speckled bird." From the stage of the Grand Ole Opry, sincere, hard-working, God-fearing people, with whom other sincere, hard-working, God-fearing people could identify, drew the performer and his audience closer to one another year by year.

Because he has experienced hardships within his own family, the rural man has always been sympathetic toward his neighbor's problems. Therefore, when in 1925 a young Kentuckian named Floyd Collins became trapped in a cave, we were concerned. Although there were 150 newspaper reporters on the scene, and one, William Miller of the Louisville *Courier-Journal*, won a Pulitzer Prize for his reporting on the tragedy, the Opry listener was much more moved by the lamenting of *The Ballad of Floyd Collins*. We listened carefully to *The Wreck of the Ole 97* as it told of a tragic 1903 Southern Railway accident in which 13 people were killed. And although many of us had never heard of Joan Crawford, F. Scott Fitzgerald, or Charles Lindbergh, names which were on the lips of the rest of America, we knew of Mary Phagan, the little factory girl who was murdered in Atlanta in 1913. The people who sang the ballads of Mary Phagan, Floyd Collins, or the Ole 97 established themselves as our friends, telling us stories from their hearts.

Numerous influences were to call us rural dwellers from the seeming security of our homes after the stock market crash of 1929, even though most of us didn't know what the stock market was. Although we were not affected by the Depression as much or as soon as the city people, we gradually began to feel the decaying of many of our established patterns. The closeness of home ties, ties to the land and to neighbors, was diminishing. The railroad called, the cities called, and the wars called—and the rural people answered them all. But as we went, we carried our music with us. Regardless of where we went, we still wanted our straightforward, non-idealistic music as a reassuring companion. Through the radio and the phonograph we were able to have it, and the tie between the Grand Ole Opry and her listeners became even stronger. Her performers became our connection to home.

A neighbor to talk to . . . that's worth a lot!

Hank Snow's "big eight-wheeler movin' down the track" meant different things to all of us. Some were leaving for good and just moving on, others were going in search of work and better living conditions; the train could get us there. The railroad became a symbol of the possible excitement on the other side of the hill, which somehow in our ever-present optimism we always wanted to see. Jimmie Rodgers had made the railroad songs prominent in the '20s, and they were to continue to be favorites for many years. From "listen to the jingle, the rumble and the roar" of *The Wabash Cannon Ball,* to the fast pace of *That Night Train to Memphis,* on to the modern versions of the *Orange Blossom Special,* the Opry has kept the railroad alive in our minds. After taking a train at the crossing or turnrow and moving to the cities, many of us have listened longingly to Roy Acuff sing "Way back in the hills as a boy I once wandered" and have thought of the peace which could be found fishing in the pond, crawfishing by the bayou, or walking up the holler at dusk.

City life wasn't always as exciting as we had anticipated, so the train also represented a way to return. Many country boys have gone to sleep in Detroit and dreamed about the cotton field and home. We have experienced the depressing shadows of city lights and spent thousands of dollars listening to records of our favorite singer reminding us of *Lamp Lighting Time in the Valley* and how the old folks were at home. Many have resolved to hop that south-bound freight and go back home, as had many of the singers who told us about it.

The train carried many of us to Nashville, because if excitement lay on the other side of the hill then it was certainly more abundant in that Tennessee town. For most of us, opportunity was and is still like the driver of the six white horses, always "comin' 'round the mountain." And we can keep our spirits up and continue to sing, because a visit to the Opry shows us that good fortune has come to many like ourselves and may come to us. If Loretta Lynn, the daughter of a poor Van Leer coal miner, can sing her way to a fortune which includes three publishing companies, one of the world's largest rodeos, a chain of western stores, a talent agency, a performing group that travels in a $100,000 tour bus, a staff of 86 employees, a home in Mazatlan, Mexico, overlooking the Gulf, and the entire town of Hurricane Mills, Tennessee, then we can keep waiting patiently for opportunity . . . and planning to have chicken and dumplin's when she comes.

Many of us who have not been content to wait for Lady Luck to come to us just know she is in Nashville . . . she *is* the Grand Ole Opry. If Loretta Lynn and Hank Williams, Roy Acuff, Webb Pierce, and Dolly Parton found opportunity in Nashville, then we want to try. After all, almost every star on the Opry has a story to tell of exchanging a homemade or cheap instrument and hand-me-downs for a jeweled guitar and glittering clothes. This Grand Ole Lady is the picture of success to us . . . if we could just get to know her. And if we can't repeat one of our hero's stories, any Saturday night we are at least able to watch an array of the images with whom we have virtually shared our lives through music.

Our heroes and our music became even more important to us during

World War II, when the uncertain road leading away to war and to the defense plants made changes in our South that would alter its entire course. In order to feel less misplaced, we again took our music with us, and WSM was most instrumental in helping.

After gaining network status in 1939, WSM could broadcast the Grand Ole Opry to all America; and we lovers of country music insisted that it be heard. We sang her songs in our barracks, we played them on our jukeboxes, and we listened to the Opry every Saturday night on radio. Hearing Bill Monroe and the Blue Grass Boys was much more important to us than listening to "Amos 'n' Andy"—to which most other Americans were dialing their oversized console radios. And while the remainder of our country preferred to "jive" to *Praise the Lord and Pass the Ammunition, This is the Army, Mr. Jones,* and *Don't Sit Under the Apple Tree with Anyone Else But Me,* we listened somberly to stories of the suffering and death of our soldiers which were being expressed by Opry stars—Roy Acuff in *Cowards Over Pearl Harbor* and *Searching for a Soldier's Grave,* Red Foley in *Smoke on the Water,* and Ernest Tubb in *The Soldier's Last Letter.* And we were not the only people in America who listened and were touched by *There's a Star Spangled Banner Waving Somewhere,* the story of a crippled boy who wanted to do his share in the war.

Although WSM had been touring many of the Grand Ole Opry performers before the war, it was perhaps its Camel Caravan in 1941 that took the Opry to more people and prominence than ever before. But more important than spreading the music, it bound even stronger the ties between that music and those of us who had been forced to try to adjust to new places, people, and ways. Seeing the entertainers and hearing them sing our favorite songs was like having a visitor from home, a friend to talk to. We knew that, as Red Foley had once remarked, "us farm boys are kinfolks . . . of the people we sing for. They're not just our fans; they're friends of ours." To us, the singers represented a neighbor to talk to us about what was happening back there. That neighborly feeling was still what we needed!

By the end of the 1940s, we had taken the Opry around the world. The Grand Ole Lady and Nashville had become synonymous with country music all over the globe. The Opry moved into the Ryman Auditorium in 1941. In 1943 the Acuff–Rose Publishing Company was founded, and in 1945 Decca began recording its country music material in WSM's Studio B. Such events definitely marked the Opry's arrival at the point of success; it had become a symbol of home, not just to us in the South but to all America, like Babe Ruth and apple pie. It is told that on the remote Pacific island of Okinawa, upon attacking a marine position, a Japanese banzai charge used a battle cry which it thought would be the ultimate in insults: "To hell with Roosevelt; to hell with Babe Ruth; to hell with Roy Acuff."

Although the Grand Ole Opry has become a very successful business, it is more significantly an institution built on a relationship between the performer and the listener. In most situations the performer has first been the listener, a lover of country music who has experienced the same happiness and sorrow which his favorite songs express. He has sat on the front porch at night and listened to the sound of whippoorwills from up in the woods and knows how it feels to be "so lonesome I could die." He has had the lovesick blues, the freight train blues, and has kept an old guitar that his uncle left behind when he went to war. He has frequented the honky-tonks, has a friend who owns or at least has driven a "semi," and probably has an Uncle Bill or Tom or Sam who has a still on the hill where he runs off a gallon or two of some of the best moonshine in the country.

The country music star has an aunt, cousin, or a sister who, very much like the sweet, innocent Minnie Pearl, is preoccupied with finding a "fel-ler," and he has been raised on a steady diet of country sunshine and Martha White biscuits. He probably has been away from home to war and lain awake in his barracks at night and thought about all these things. Because of this first-hand experience, he becomes a successful singer and is able to express sincerely those feelings which he has known. His listeners are those of us who have known these same things and therefore feel at home with such discussions. We see in country music a reflection of our life. The Grand Ole Opry has so successfully mirrored this lifestyle that it has gained her a place in our hearts rivaled only by such few precious things as God, mother, country, and home.

Roy Acuff and the Smoky Mountain Boys . . .

Roy understood our plight . . .

As we sought to make a living out of black land dirt.

We lived a simple way of life that's fading . . .

Entertained each other at home . . .

And away.

Neighbors "joined in" at the slightest opportunity.

We were caring neighbors from down the lane.

Opry performers reassured us "there's a better home awaitin' in the sky."

Suddenly, outside influences began calling us from the security of our land.

We waited at the crossing . . .

To board that "big eight wheeler" . . .

That would move us to the cities.

War called and we rural people answered . . .

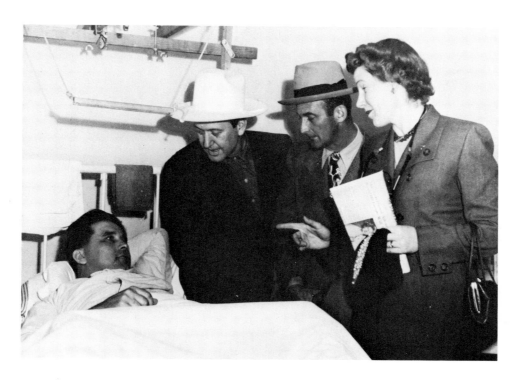

*Opry stars like Red Foley, Rod Brasfield,
and our beloved Minnie Pearl visited our wounded.*

*Performers like Pee Wee King and his Golden West Cowboys (left) and
Eddy Arnold (center) traveled the country over with the Camel Caravan.*

How we missed our country sunshine, Martha White Biscuits . . .

Banjo pickin' on the back porch . . .

And the green, green sounds of home.

CHAPTER II

It's a long trip
... but worth it!

TO those of us who live around Big Stone Gap, Virginia, some things are as regular as milking twice a day. One of those things is listening to the Grand Ole Opry on Saturday night, and we have listened regularly ever since it began. Occasionally, but not often, we get a chance to go to Nashville to see the Opry; when we get that chance it is something special because it means more to us than some people can imagine. We're from Carter Family country, where the *Wildwood Flower* actually grows along the fence row, where *My Clinch Mountain Home* is reality with weather-beaten boards, where *Coal Miner's Blues* isn't just a song but a feeling, and where *Bury Me Under the Weeping Willow* is often the most comforting hope of a weary life.

We're not far from Bristol, the setting of perhaps the most important recording event in country music history—the two-day Carter Family —Jimmie Rodgers original recording session. Not far across into Kentucky is Lynch, and then Harlan, and then Hyden—the scene of a mining disaster for which Loretta Lynn and many other Opry stars raised $91,000. We live in the heart of what the government calls Appalachia, which we are told is America's richest region in terms of natural resources. Conversely, we are also told by statistics that we are "the poorest and most illiterate populace in the United States, suffering from poverty, disease, and deprivation to an extent that is alien to the official and highly advertised 'American Way of Life.' "

We are part of an area covering 257 counties on the Appalachian Mountain range which is home to about 8 million people. To most of America, Appalachia is merely a setting for moonshine stills, family feuds, and Li'l Abner, but to us it has always been a refuge where we could maintain a cherished separateness and independence in our way of life. Our lives are often hard and beset with failure, but we have adjusted to that; because of our hardships, we have learned to look forward to eternal salvation instead of earthly reward.

Thoughts of life and death have always been the subject of our music, and the home of our music is the Grand Ole Opry. Opry performers are our heroes—people like us who have achieved success and we are proud of them. We have to save for a long time to make the trip to Nashville, but witnessing Loretta Lynn sing *I Was Born a Coal Miner's Daughter* makes us proud and the wait worthwhile.

It used to be difficult to drive out of Appalachia since we hardly ever had new cars, and our roads were winding and narrow. But with TVA, Alcoa, and Oak Ridge reaching into our area, we now have access to interstate highways. By following Highway 23 through Kingsport we come to I-81, and then before getting to Knoxville we junction with I-40 which takes us all the way to Nashville.

As we drive along we notice many reminders of country music success—a sign identifying Sevierville, a hometown celebrating "Dolly Parton Day" every year; Highway 33 cutting through to Maynardsville, the home of Roy Acuff and Carl Smith; Radio WNOX, Knoxville, the station which gave many of the Opry stars their first opportunity to be heard by the public; Cass Walker on the radio, which means country music in east Tennessee; and, of course, Tennessee itself!

Tennessee mountains are similar to ours since they are still part of Appalachia, but the scene changes a great deal after we leave the Cumberland Plateau. Although recent years have found 40 percent of the families in this state with incomes of less than $3,000, the U.S. Department of Commerce now reports that, in per capita income, Tennessee is the fastest growing state in the fastest growing region in the United States. The major factor for this growth has been the Tennessee Valley Authority which Congress established in 1935. Power made available by TVA was one reason why the government established the atomic project at Oak Ridge.

Most of the state's better farmland is in the southern portion where its leading crop, cotton, is grown. But although three-fourths of Tennessee is farmland, less than one-half of its population live on farms or have agricultural occupations related to producing crops and livestock. Yet it is still ranked as the Jersey cattle center of the nation. Tennessee is noted for many other bonuses—the 500,000-acre Great Smoky Mountains National Park, Memphis and its Beale Street blues, Tennessee walking horses, Elvis Presley, Pat Boone, Tennessee Ernie Ford, Dinah Shore, and its three presidents, Andrew Jackson, James K. Polk, and Andrew Johnson. But to us, and we suspect to a majority of other Americans, it's mostly noted for the Grand Ole Opry and Nashville, "Music City, U.S.A."

We have been coming to Nashville every time we could afford it since the Grand Ole Opry started in 1925, and we have noticed a lot of changes. In the mid-1920s the city was basically agriculturally oriented, the poultry center of the South. Nashville's butter-making industry churned over 4 million pounds annually, and she produced more snuff than any other southern city. However, even then Nashville was becoming an industrial center. She published more religious periodicals and literature than any other city in the nation; in volume of business, investment, and number of employees, her printing industry was larger than any two cities in the South combined. More soft collars were manufactured here than in any other city in the South, and she produced 90 percent of the coffee cans used in the area.

But Nashville's most famous attraction in the '20s was the Maxwell House Hotel, and the city's most famous product was Maxwell House Coffee, created by Cheek–Neal Coffee Company of Nashville. The hotel is now memory. After it burned, the property for which Colonel John Overton paid about $15 in 1855 was sold for $1.4 million in 1961, and the 20-story Third National Bank building now stands in its place. But its name lives on through the internationally known coffee which bears its name because millions in this world believe, as did Theodore Roosevelt when he visited Nashville, that it's "good to the last drop." The Cheek family is remembered through the 55-acre Cheekwood estate, featuring a 60-room Georgian mansion, which now serves the area as Tennessee Botanical Gardens and Fine Arts Center.

Located 220 miles southeast of the United States center of population, Nashville publicizes that she is within 600 miles of 50 percent of the residents of America and within 1,000 miles of 70 percent. With this central location at the crossroads of three interstate highways (one of only five or six cities in the nation sharing this distinction), Music City, U.S.A. could not be in a better position for growth. And she *has* grown! The first time we came here in 1925, her population was near 150,000 while today it is almost 500,000. Of course, since 1963, when the metropolitan government was established, Nashville's population has included all of Davidson County.

Aside from growth as a music center, Nashville has grown in many other ways. Since the mid-1800s, a printing center has prospered here. Today this industry ranks in the top twenty among American cities, with its commercial printers alone having 1973 sales exceeding $130 million. Over 250 printing businesses, publishers, and suppliers which have over 9,000 employees and an annual payroll of over $53 million are located here. In one year, the U.S. Post Office stated that 75 percent of the mail processed from Nashville was publications; only five cities in the nation mail more publications. It also estimated that 35 to 40 percent of this volume was classified as some type of religious publication.

The religious publications industry was started because Nashville was a city with numerous churches and schools. Now it is a city of over 720 churches and has the twenty-sixth largest public school system in the country. This is a city of 14 colleges and universities, including Vanderbilt University, which is ranked in that 10 percent of American universities performing the overwhelming majority of research done in the United States. Also included are two famous predominantly black colleges—Fisk University and Meharry Medical College. In 1920 when the U.S. government recognized as colleges only three institutions for higher education for the Negro, two of these were Fisk and Meharry. Both grew to great prominence, and today Meharry is the only privately supported predominantly Negro medical college in the nation, having graduated about one-half of the country's black physicians and dentists during its first 85 years.

Today Meharry annually receives over 4,000 applications for its 112 enrollment places.

Of course Nashville has numerous industries other than printing and publishing. The city's Ford plant is the world's largest auto glass plant. Also located here is Genesco, the world's largest and most diversified producer and retailer of wearing apparel and footwear. The Nashville division of Peterbilt Motor Company, which produces heavy-duty truck tractors, is Tennessee's only automotive manufacturing plant. Almost 700 industrial establishments have made Nashville a new city.

Nestled in the midst of the city's burgeoning growth is one of Nashville's most significant historical landmarks, the Ryman Auditorium. There will be about 6.2 million tourists in Nashville this year who will be inspired by the beauty of Andrew Jackson's Hermitage and awed by Belle Meade, the first thoroughbred racing farm in America. And though we will be fascinated by the numerous historical homes and impressed with Nashville's exact replica of the Parthenon, to many of us, the most impressive landmark will be the Ryman Auditorium.

The history of this antiquated, barn-like auditorium reveals to us the likes and dislikes of Nashvillians since 1891—the programs they supported and financed, the speakers to whom they listened, and the entertainers they preferred. Of moving significance is the fact that within these walls many of our heroes became heroes and as a result made country music and Nashville internationally known. We were here in 1941 when the Opry moved in. That was the year after Minnie Pearl joined the show and Bill Monroe and Roy Acuff were relatively new, but the Ryman was already known all over America.

Mrs. Lula C. Naff had managed the building since 1914 and had brought it to the attention of the entertainment world. Katherine Cornell had termed it "one of the most picturesque institutions in America and much more interesting than the replica of the Parthenon." *Variety* later proclaimed it "the most famous one-night stand on the road." And now it was to be the home of the Grand Ole Opry, which would bring it more publicity than all its previous attractions.

As the years passed, we came back time after time, and the Ryman came to mean everything to us; it became a sanctuary where we could cast off our burdens. The old tabernacle gave us peace. When we waited in line outside, we felt as if we knew everyone else because we all were excited about the same thing. Once we were even tempted to give up our reserved seats to some folks who had driven from Michigan and then couldn't get tickets. When we got inside, the excitement made us feel like we were back home at the fairground or a big tent-meeting. And we were there on the last night the Opry performed in the Ryman before moving to the new Grand Ole Opry House, and although we wanted the new home, we were glad when Minnie Pearl broke down and cried . . . then we could do the same.

Now we're back in Nashville, and we feel that we must drop in and greet our old friend who has shown us so many good times; it's like going back to the old home place. The vacant building is like an empty grandstand after the program is over. But we have been here so often that our memories can fill it with special events. Hank Williams is standing on the stage at his first appearance here in June, 1949. Even the program hawkers stop and listen to *Lovesick Blues* because we all know that another country boy has reached the top—from selling peanuts to singing at the Grand Ole Opry. Finally, after Hank sings six encores, Red Foley comes to the microphone to quiet the audience or we would clap all night. A chapter within itself . . . written by two great stars in an old history book that's being discarded. The new book will list these people's influence but such events will give way to newer happenings.

As we tour the Ryman, our guide tells us that this was originally the Union Gospel Tabernacle built for the great revivalist Sam Jones and that such preachers as Billy Sunday and William Jennings Bryan spoke from that stage. Behind her voice we seem to hear Porter Wagoner delivering *If Jesus Came to Your House,* one of the best sermons we ever heard. She tells us that most of the great dancers of the world have danced here—Isadora Duncan, Anna Pavlova, and the incomparable Nijinski; we hear the tapping of the Stoney Mountain Cloggers square-dancing to the Crook Brothers as they play *Arkansas Traveler.*

While the tour guide mentions that the great French actress Sarah Bernhardt has performed on that stage, as well as Pauline Frederick, Geraldine Farrar, and Helen Hayes, we relive the nights when Rod Brasfield would tease Minnie Pearl about her Uncle Nabob, causing us to forget that we had barely enough gas money to get us back to Virginia the next day. The guide continues to tell us that this auditorium has been filled with the sounds of such great opera singers as Enrico Caruso and Amelita Galli-Curci; we hear the haunting sound of Patsy Cline singing *I Fall to Pieces* . . . and then Jim Reeves singing *Four Walls.* Although we duly note that such great violinists as Mischa Elman and Fritz Kreisler have played here, we can't imagine anyone outfiddling Roy Acuff. Paderewski played the piano there on that stage; we wonder if his piano was an upright with the front removed.

The guide tells us Tom Ryman's funeral was held in this building, since he had been the force behind its construction, and on that day the auditorium was draped with black. We feel the absence of David "Stringbean" Akeman on the night the Opry was stopped for a minute in remembrance of this marvelous performer who had been murdered along with his wife. We relive the shock of the night when Hank Williams' death was announced. We feel the absence of Red Foley, Jim Reeves, Patsy Cline, Hawkshaw Hawkins, Tex Ritter . . . no funeral drapings could have added to the sadness.

While the guide continues, we sit in one of the long church pews installed in the 1890s and survey the empty building. We have never seen it empty before. As we look around, our memories fill the pews with hometown folks: a couple and their three little children, fanning with their programs, smiling at Jimmy Dickens singing *Sleeping at the Foot of the Bed*; an old man wearing a flannel shirt nodding his head to the beat of Grandpa Jones' banjo and *Here Rattler Here*; two newly-weds snuggled together contentedly listening as Tammy Wynette sings *D-I-V-O-R-C-E* . . . and many other faces . . . but gradually they fade. . . .

We have never noticed the initials carved on the backs and arms of the pews and the chewing gum stuck beneath, but now they seem to be memoranda of times that had escaped our memory. Glancing over our shoulders, we notice the old windows with sunlight shining through on the ancient pews and scarred floor . . . the picture looks so much like our little church back home, magnified about ten times. How appropriate that this building has been called "the Mother Church of Country Music." The sounds of Red Foley singing *Precious Memories* drift through our recollections—"how they linger . . . how they ever flood my soul." And they are precious!

We return to reality as our tour guide opens the door and we step out into the glaring light of Nashville's Fifth Avenue. As we pass the familiar alley between the auditorium and Tootsie's Orchid Lounge, we remember watching Webb Pierce arrive in his Pontiac, its interior incrusted with silver dollars. But we go to our car and drive the nine miles to Opryland, U.S.A. and the new Grand Ole Opry House, and all the precious memories of the past thirty years are engulfed by the excitement of the present. Naturally we bought our tickets in advance through the mail—as do some 3,400 each week—or we wouldn't be able to get in. Although the new auditorium seats 4,400, it still takes two shows each Saturday night, a Saturday matinee during the summer months, and a Friday night Opry from February through November to begin to accommodate the crowd.

When we approach the new Opry House we are amazed. A concrete shingled tile roof sloping down in three directions makes it look like the most elaborate barn we've ever seen. And the closer we get the more elaborate it looks! The heavy wood slab doors with large metal straps and exposed bolts make it appear even more massive. Inside, under the 21-foot-high wood-beamed ceiling, we can buy programs, popcorn, and cokes, just like we could at the Ryman. Of course, the facilities are much more modern.

We are told that the new $15 million building is an "elaborate and tasteful reincarnation of the old Ryman—in concrete and brick, steel and wood, with cushioned church-pew type seats." But although it does not remind us of the old home, it is our new home and it's as if we had always been here.

When Hank Snow comes on stage and sings *I Don't Hurt Anymore,* the stage is larger, but that only allows more space around it for visitors to illuminate his glittering clothes with flash cameras. Dolly Parton sings *Sacred Memories* ("when I got baptized they sang *Amazing Grace*"), and her lines remind us of our experiences in the little church outside Big Stone Gap and of our hopes of being able to afford a new one.

It's a long trip . . . but worth it!

The thought helps to clarify our happy feelings about this new auditorium. We've left beloved Ryman and have moved into this new place, but we're still in "the Mother Church of Country Music" because the Grand Ole Opry is not a building—it's a communication . . . a state of mind . . . a Grand Ole Lady in her finest hour.

Those of us from around Big Stone Gap, Virginia, listen to the Grand Ole Opry as regularly as milking twice a day.

The Opry has been our relief from the burdens of a hard life.

So over a period of time, we saved up enough by making chairs . . .

Or hooking rugs, to make the trip to Nashville to see the Opry first hand.

On our way, we saw reminders of country music success,
like the Dolly Parton Day celebration in Sevierville . . .

Majestic mansions lining our route
as we neared "Music City, USA."

Our Saturdays were full when we visited the "Athens of the South."
The exact reproduction of the Parthenon gave us a chance
to see Greece at home.

Although we knew we would never own one, mansions were always a source of hope, inspiration, and incentive. Mansions like Belle Meade. . .

And Oaklands.

Early Saturday afternoon,
we hurried to the Ryman Auditorium, home of the Opry
for thirty-three years . . . (center triangle).

There we lined up for tickets
for that night's performance.

Some who had driven
hundreds of miles
could not get in.

Although world-famed entertainers
like Fritz Kreisler had appeared at the Ryman . . .

We were more interested in Grandpa Jones,
who performed and carried on like our Uncle Prather.

Paderewski had played here, but we didn't know him.

On the other hand, we raised the roof when Roy Acuff came out fiddlin'.

Pauline Frederick may have been an outstanding Mary of Scotland . . .

But Minnie Pearl was our queen at the Ryman . . .

And Hank Williams became a living legend.

Ryman performers
Helen Hayes, Geraldine Farrar,
and Amelita Galli-Curci
all attained world-wide renown . . .

But Dolly Parton and Tammy Wynette were our superstars.

Red Foley and Tex Ritter were our idols.

*If Henry VIII had appeared in royal robes, he would
have been upstaged by Hank Snow in his glittering outfit.*

We have been back to the Opry, this last time at the new Opryland.
And we are pleased that the neighborly feeling is still there . . .
the communication, the state of mind . . .
the Grand Ole Lady is in her finest hour.

The Opry in Color

Neighborliness, a spontaneous country music ingredient, is vividly demonstrated between Roy Acuff and Grandpa Jones.

Neighbors to the Governor of Tennessee, the Webb Pierces relax beside their guitar-shaped swimming pool.

One of the best-known Opry stars, Sara Ophelia Cannon, better known as Cousin Minnie Pearl, also resides next door to the Tennessee Governor's Mansion.

Texan Charlie Walker, a former disc jockey, joined the Opry in 1967.

Resounding notes from Houston's Barbara Mandrell belie her diminutive stature.

Stonewall Jackson, a native of Moultrie, Georgia, has sung with the Opry since 1954.

Maybelle Carter, the "Queen Mother of Country Music."

A $15 million structure, the new Grand Ole Opry House continues to reign as the Mother Church of Country Music. It is part of a $28 million, 369-acre amusement park that annually attracts some 1.7 million visitors to Nashville.

The new Grand Ole Opry House, "an elaborate and tasteful reincarnation of the old Ryman."

The Roy Acuff Museum in Opryland.

CHAPTER III

From the beginning ... it was always worth waiting in line

"WHY shucks, a man don't get warmed up in an hour," was the feeling of Uncle Jimmy Thompson on November 28, 1925, when he finished the first program of what was later to become the Grand Ole Opry. And most fans agreed . . . to the point that within fifteen years it grew to a 4½-hour program on Nashville's WSM radio. WSM allowed the Opry to grow, and it gave growth to WSM.

In less than two months after it went on the air on October 5, 1925, as a 1,000-watt channel, WSM, the broadcasting station of the National Life and Accident Insurance Company, introduced a hillbilly radio show called the WSM Barn Dance. Launching the show in Studio A was the station's first director, George D. Hay, whom we all came to know as the Solemn Old Judge. Hay was a man who could visualize the impact that such a program might have on the relatively new medium called radio.

In the 1920s, radio became a phenomenon; its sales went from less than $2 million in 1920 to more than $600 million by 1929. Although the movie and recording industries also saw considerable growth during this period, those of us outside the cities knew little about them. But radio reached into all our homes, talking to many of us who had never seen a movie and could not afford the luxury of phonograph records and Victrolas. And once it reached into our homes it began featuring our music. WLS in Chicago was the first station to feature a barn dance program, but was followed quickly by others; WSM's presentation has outlasted them all. Since November, 1925, it has become the longest continuous radio program ever presented in America, having been interrupted only occasionally by a Franklin D. Roosevelt "fireside chat" during World War II.

After the first hour-long program of fiddling, interest began to build, and it was only a few weeks before string bands from around Nashville asked to join in. They did . . . in abundance. The first was Dr. Humphrey Bates of Vanderbilt University and a group of his neighbors, referred to as "the Possum Hunters." Then came such groups as the Crook Brothers, the Gulley Jumpers, the Fruit Jar Drinkers, and the Dixieliners. Their music was as down-to-earth as their names. They were country neighbors picking "fiddlin' tunes" they liked to play.

FIFTY YEARS AT THE GRAND OLE OPRY

The first Barn Dance entertainers were chiefly pickers. Although occasionally a singer was featured, the type of music we wanted was dancing music; it was a vital part of our life when neighbors got together. On the other hand, our songs were personal—a song that Daddy sang as he plowed behind a mule, or a song that Mama crooned while she rocked Brother to sleep. Such songs were too intimate for us to sing before a microphone; most country people were too self-conscious. It took a professional entertainer to "let 'er go." Uncle Dave Macon was just that—a first-rate comic, an old hand at playing the vaudeville and minstrel shows, and an extraordinary five-string banjo player. By the time he joined the WSM program in 1926 there were about 25 in the cast, but Uncle Dave was its chief singing star for many years.

While Uncle Dave was stomping his foot, shouting, and singing such songs as *Rock About My Sara Jane* and *Bully of the Town* every Saturday night, WSM was hearing the echoes and realizing a tremendous growth. Those of us who love country music were accustomed to taking part in breakdowns; those who sat around on the floor, or whatever space was available, and patted their feet and clapped their hands were just as important as the fiddler. We wanted to take part at the Opry, too, so WSM invited us . . . never thinking that so many of us would actually come. The cast itself had grown so much that more space was needed, so in Studio B, additional area was provided for 50 to 60 visitors. When WSM began to send its performers out touring the surrounding areas, this whetted our appetites even more. We began to converge on the station on Saturday nights, and this brought about Studio C, which accommodated about 500 fans.

The Grand Ole Opry, which had been named such in 1926 by George Hay, grew by leaps and bounds, and so did WSM. Both were helped by the tremendous growth of radio. The Depression and the unemployment of 13–15 million people (25 percent of the labor force) obviously affected all areas of American life. However, it was estimated that by 1929, there was already one radio in every three homes, and we could now listen to them at no extra cost. So the radio became even more important. It was described as "a pervading and somewhat God-like presence" which had come into the lives and homes of the country. Radio grew. And WSM grew . . . and grew; but its own child was about to engulf it.

Because the Opry's fans had grown to such large numbers and their loyalty was bringing them *en masse* to Nashville, it was necessary that even more space be provided. This led to WSM's decision to find a location outside its studio; the size of the audience was making it difficult to operate the station. The Opry was moved to a local theatre, the Hillsboro, located at Hillsboro Road and Acklen Avenue. Even though it began to schedule two performances every Saturday night, all of us still could not get in. In 1937 we followed it to the Dixie Tabernacle on Fatherland Street in east Nashville, but there were still too many of us.

In 1939, the Federal Communications Commission designated certain frequencies, including WSM, as clear channels; this meant that the station could be received without interference as far as its signal could reach. WSM built what was then the nation's largest tower—871 feet, increased its power to 50,000 watts, and billed itself as the "Air Castle of the South." It could then be heard at many points all over the nation and in some parts of Canada. In January of that year, R. J. Reynolds Tobacco Company sponsored a half-hour portion of the Opry to advertise its Prince Albert smoking tobacco. This segment was placed on the NBC Red Network with 26 stations receiving it.

The next year, on July 20, 1940, 35 NBC stations began carrying the Prince Albert program, and it was heard from coast-to-coast. Thus, the sounds and neighborly feeling of the Grand Ole Opry reached all America . . . and it seemed as if all of us wanted to be part of it, too. Increasing numbers came to Nashville to visit the Opry. The program was moved to the new War Memorial Auditorium which seated 2,200, and an admission fee of 25 cents was charged. Strange as it may seem, the admission fee was an effort to limit attendance!

But attendance was not to be limited. Through the 1930s, such additional performers as the Vagabonds, Zeke Clements, Sarie and Sally, Robert Lunn (the talking blues man), Curley Fox (the champion fiddler), and Pee Wee King and his Golden West Cowboys had become a part of our lives. And when Roy Acuff joined the cast in 1938, the Opry began a new period of growth. Previously there had been mainly bands, which featured singers taking selections from our established folk music. Now there were singers whose billing overshadowed that of the bands. With Acuff on the stage, it seemed as if nothing could limit the audience.

In this prewar and post-Depression era, the nation was spending more money than ever before, more even than it had. When "Gone with the Wind" premiered in Atlanta in 1939, it was America's greatest and most expensive movie ever. And even before the New York World's Fair opened in April of the same year, it had cost more than $150 million. We country music fans would certainly pay 25 cents to see our idols at the Grand Ole Opry.

In 1940, the Opry was 15 years old and had already outgrown all its homes. Yet in the next fifteen years it was to see growth that would be much more astounding . . . growth that would make its stars not only wealthy but internationally famous . . . growth that would build multimillion-dollar businesses for WSM and Nashville.

Perhaps one of the reasons for that growth was that the Opry had finally found a home, a building with which it could be identified. In 1941, the performance moved into Nashville's Ryman Auditorium which housed the Opry for more than thirty succeeding years. The Ryman had been built as a large tabernacle for religious meetings, and its almost circular seating arrangement gave the audience a closeness even though it accommodated over 3,500 people.

With the rise of the singing star, the great shift in population that was about to take place in America, and the increased advertising through radio and touring, listenership grew day by day. Roy Acuff began to create material to fit his own style; *The Wreck on the Highway* and *The Wabash Cannon Ball* brought out Acuff's personality as well as a message or story. Songwriters began to emerge who would write tailor-made lyrics for individual singers. When Eddy Arnold, a guitar player and singer with Pee Wee King's band, found *Mommy, Please Stay Home with Me*, he found stardom.

By selecting material suited to their styles, other singers became immediate successes, and the Grand Ole Opry "star system" was under way. Ernest Tubb used *I'm Walking the Floor Over You;* for Red Foley it was *Smoke on the Water.* Cowboy Copas became identified with *Philipino Baby,* George Morgan with *Candy Kisses,* and little Jimmy Dickens with *Old Cold 'Tater.* Hank Williams was known for *Lovesick Blues* and Hank Snow for *I'm Movin' On.* Particular songs, along with appearances on the Grand Ole Opry, also made other stars between 1940 and 1955—Carl Smith, Ray Price, Faron Young, Webb Pierce, Kitty Wells, and Hawkshaw Hawkins, to name a few.

During this period we also saw the rapid rise of a number of nonsinging stars. When Sara Ophelia Colley joined the cast of the Opry in 1940 as Minnie Pearl, she began a trend of solo comics. Cousin Minnie was a person with whom we rural listeners could identify, as were Lonzo and Oscar, Rod Brasfield, and the Duke of Paducah. Although previously a comic character had been featured with numerous bands, only a few of them had performed solo. As the comedy stars increased at the Opry so did the audience.

With each star came a style, and these styles effected dramatic changes in the Opry. One such innovation was honky-tonk music. During the Depression, saloons and taverns had taken on a new significance in the lives of many rural people. These whiskey parlors, which we called honky-tonks, were located just outside the cities because the tax rates were lower there, police interference was less likely, and both city and rural folk could be served. They became gathering places for many farmers, laborers, truck drivers, and displaced rural dwellers to whom country music had been a way of life. The honky-tonk music reflected the problems of those of us who sat at the tables, leaned on the bars, and stared into the jukeboxes . . . people who were dejected and down-and-out.

The songs became even more frank and realistic, dealing with subjects that no other music form would mention—drinking, divorce, infidelity, marital problems, and tragedy. Such songs as *Driving Nails in My Coffin* and *Headin' Down the Wrong Highway* talked straight to the noisy, boisterous, honky-tonk drinkers. This noisy crowd created another change—in order for the music to be heard, the performer needed to amplify his instruments. This more personal subject matter and the amplification of instruments began to change the sound of the Opry, especially through many of its songwriters. Ernest Tubb, one of the first Opry singers to use the new instruments, started a trend that by the end of the 1940s was the dominant sound at the Opry.

From the beginning . . . it was always worth waiting in line

One of the major American attractions of the 1930s had been the singing cowboy movies. Although the first western stars had dressed as hard-working ranch hands, rapidly the image changed to the fancy-dressed, guitar-totin' cowboy on a beautiful horse. This image became such a symbol throughout all America that Hopalong Cassidy clothes had grossed $40 million by 1950. The music the cowboy sang was almost identical to ours; the stories just took place on the prairies of Texas instead of the hills of Virginia. Many of our country music singers began to be influenced by this western hero—they took western names, wore western clothes, and some even sang about life on the prairies although they had never been west of the Mississippi. And the Opry fan began to expect jeweled clothes, cowboy boots, and 10-gallon hats to go along with such names as the Singing Ranger, the Golden West Cowboys, and the Texas Troubadour. By the end of the 1940s, almost everyone on the Opry had adopted something western in their acts.

Perhaps the biggest influence ever on country music, and therefore on the Grand Ole Opry, was the shift in population which resulted from America's entry into World War II. Although some of us from the rural South had begun to move into the nearby cities during the Depression, it was not until the war that we began to move into the North. With us we took our music. Although at first the city folk did not accept it, it was not long before our music was popular at service training centers and on defense plant assembly lines.

With nearly 16 million people joining the armed forces from Pearl Harbor Day to V-J Day, a great part of America was away from home. And since we were such loyal fans, country music's popularity increased. Lonely people used music to connect them to home and its coveted ways, and we seemed more lonely than others. Where country music went, the Grand Ole Opry went; and where the Opry went, its stars soon toured. Jukebox business was at a record high; it was an $80-million, 400,000-box business. The boxes were taking in 5 billion nickels yearly and a big percentage of those were on country music; jukebox operators reported that country hits remained popular long after a "pop" song had faded. The Grand Ole Opry became more and more a focal point for us; it was a thing which we shared with folks back home. It presented music and people with whom we could identify.

The Opry developed a vast and responsive listening audience which was of great interest to advertisers. Businesses concerned with selling products that were popular with country folks—Black Draught, Wine of Cardui, Garrett Snuff, Stevens Work Clothes, Royal Crown Cola, or Light Crust Flour—realized the potential in radio advertising and even began sending groups to tour surrounding areas to promote their products. They found that we rural fans were not only loyal to our favorite performers but also to the products they advertised.

Since 1939, Prince Albert had sponsored a 30-minute segment of the Opry for NBC. In 1941 the company helped send the Camel Caravan, a unit of 20, on a tour of 50,000 miles to entertain servicemen. Warren Paint

FIFTY YEARS AT THE GRAND OLE OPRY

Company found that by advertising on the Opry it increased its dealerships in the central South by 83 percent; O'Bryan Brothers' advertising on the Opry increased its sales 24 percent in two years, although it had been in business for eighty-five years. General Shoe Corporation bought a half-hour pre-Opry show time to advertise its Cedarcrest work shoes and watched sales increase 96 percent in two years. And to test WSM audience interest at a different hour than its regular program, Jefferson Island Salt bought a one-minute spot announcement for one time only at 7:00 P.M. in September, 1951, and offered a free picture of little Jimmy Dickens who starred on its regular portion of the Opry; the company received over 24,000 replies.

By 1950, the name "Grand Ole Opry" meant country music to the world. It had a cast of about 120, including sidemen and comedians. All other barn dance programs had become insignificant compared to this one; they served merely as stepping stones on the glory road to the Opry. And they served well for such stars as Hank Williams, Webb Pierce, Slim Whitman, Jim Reeves, Kitty Wells, Faron Young, and others. But the Grand Ole Opry was the center of country music . . . the ultimate, the top of the mountain, the end of the rainbow for which every country music performer searched.

By mid-century, the honky-tonk beat had practically taken over. Kitty Wells earned the title of "Queen of Country Music" because of her great success with *It Wasn't God Who Made Honky-tonk Angels,* and Floyd Tillman had become very popular because of his hit, *Slipping Around.*

Hank Snow and Hank Williams were idols of the Opry, wearing fancy western clothes to fit the image we wanted to see. In the fall of 1951, business was so good that WSM initiated the Friday Night Frolic, a program using the Opry stars and giving another chance to those of us who had trouble getting tickets for the Saturday night shows. The Opry had grown to towering heights. However, it was about to experience a period of change that would affect it, the city of Nashville, and the world more than could have been imagined in 1940.

As in the early 1940s, when the rise of the singing star had changed our traditional songs, this new period too would alter the country sound. As in the 1930s, when honky-tonk music brought electrified instruments onto the Opry stage, this new period would likewise affect instrumentation. And just as the popularity of the stars and recording industry began to commercialize the Opry in the early 1940s, this new period would commercialize it even more. But just as in the previous changes, when there were people who were determined to maintain its direct and straightforward way of communication and neighborly flavor, this new period would have people dedicated to the same goals.

In the mid-1950s, America was hit by rock-and-roll. The most noticeable strike was made by a southerner, Elvis Presley, whose intermingling of country and rhythm and blues launched a new era in American music history. His showmanship and personality were especially effective during a period when a teenage record-buying population was demanding youth and a discussion of their own interests.

On the Opry, the bulk of the stars still held to a steady flow of old-time songs, but some began to modify their styles to attract a larger following. Prior to this time, records had been bought primarily by adults, and Ernest Tubb, Kitty Wells, and Roy Acuff were their favorites. But the majority of Americans in the mid-1950s were under 25 years of age, and everything being sold was directed to this group. They had a different outlook on life and were not particularly interested in songs about mother and country; country music had to appeal to this group or give way to music that did. The result? A new music which combined rock-and-roll and country; some called it "rockabilly." Sonny James' *Young Love* was neither country nor rock-and-roll, but it appealed to youth.

Other country music singers began to realize the importance of selling to teenagers and as a result such performers as the Everly Brothers, Marty Robbins, Jim Reeves, Don Gibson, Faron Young, Ferlin Huskey, Patsy Cline, and Johnny Cash altered country music dramatically. They took these changes onto the stage of the Opry, and drums and backup groups soon became familiar fixtures there. Still, many refused to alter their simplicity, and such stars as Porter Wagoner, Wilma Lee and Stoney Cooper, Hank Snow, and others remained favorites of the pure country music fan. However, all of America's music was forced to acknowledge the younger generation, and the Opry changed considerably because of it.

Seeing such trends as threats to country music, the Country Music Association was organized in 1948 for the purpose of improving, marketing, and publicizing country music. That it did! It worked to establish more radio stations dedicated to its music. From 1961 to 1966, the number of full-time country radio stations increased from 81 to 328. The CMA, by stimulating the great commercial upsurge and worldwide expansion of country music during the 1960s, helped the Grand Ole Opry to continue its growth.

On November 12, 1971, construction began on the Grand Ole Opry's long awaited permanent home—the first auditorium built especially for the Opry. Although the Ryman Auditorium had been home for thirty years, the Opry had long ago outgrown it and needed a place that would comfortably accommodate its nearly one million annual visitors. On March 16, 1974, the $15 million Grand Ole Opry House opened at Opryland, U.S.A., with a house full of visiting dignitaries, including the president of the United States.

Now when Rodney and Hazel Herndon from Baxley, Georgia, save their money and travel 475 miles (approximately the average distance for the Opry visitor), they hear Tammy Wynette and George Jones singing *We're Gonna Hold On* from the stage of one of the largest auditoriums in the nation and the largest radio and television broadcasting studio in the world. They sit in air-conditioned comfort and are surrounded by a brick and wood design conducive to maintaining the rustic feeling of the Opry.

They remember their previous visit to the Ryman Auditorium in 1963 and the feeling they experienced from knowing that Hank Williams sang on this stage. Hazel likes the new place better when she reads in the *WSM Grand Ole Opry History-Picture Book* that a disk of flooring six feet in diameter was actually removed from the floor of the Ryman stage and inset into the new Grand Ole Opry House. The new house is just an extension of the old one, making the Grand Ole Opry "just a little bigger . . . just a little better."

WSM's *first studio, 1925.*

Uncle Dave Macon and WSM's *first director, George D. Hay,*
the "Solemn Old Judge" who named the Grand Ole Opry in 1926.

Paul Warmack and His Gully Jumpers.

Arthur Smith and The Dixie Liners.

Ryman Auditorium before it became the home of the Grand Ole Opry.

*Roy Acuff, "Mr. Opry," joined the cast in 1938
as a singer with a band.*

When Sara Ophelia Cannon (nee Colley) joined the Opry in 1940 as Minnie Pearl, an era of solo comics began.

During World War II, she traveled to hospitals . . .

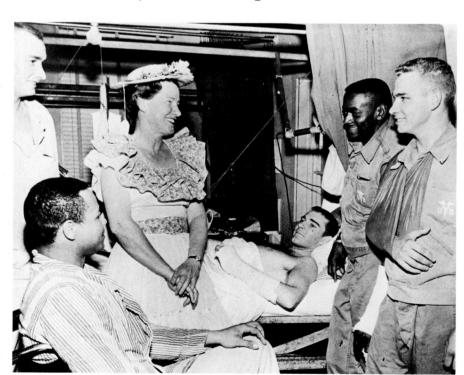

USO entertainment centers . . .

*All over Europe. Photographed here in Germany with Red Foley,
Minnie gives chocolate to a child.*

The Willis Brothers, without Skeeter.

CHAPTER IV

We made music
that was different
...but worth millions of dollars!

WHEN we first started coming to Nashville in the 1920s, our music was new to everyone except those of us who had shelled peas to the rhythm of a fiddle or who had boiled and eaten peanuts while listening to a string band pickin' on the porch. Others who had heard it ignored it because it was flavored with our language patterns which often were considered to be a mark of near-illiteracy.

Besides, the rest of America had its mind on other things—like great sports events. In 1920, Man O' War won the greatest horse race ever; in 1924, Johnny Weissmuller set the world swimming record for the 100-meter race at the Olympics; in 1926, Gertrude Ederle swam the English Channel; in 1927, Babe Ruth hit 60 home runs, and Jack Dempsey and Gene Tunney had the fight of the decade. America was in love with its sports stars. The country was also in love with its movie idols. From 1922 to 1929, weekly attendance at movies doubled from 40 million to 89 million. America was too involved in other things to pay attention to the music we were making in the rural South.

The only attention America did give us was out of need. The Prohibition Act of 1920 made the city people sit up and take notice of our ability to make one thing—moonshine. They made it sound respectable by reasoning that we had been taught the art by our forefathers who had brought the knowledge and a love of drinking over from the old country. But wherever it came from, we had it; and we soon found that our jugs and fruitjars couldn't hold enough for the demand from such big cities as Chicago, Detroit, and New York.

It might have been through this commerce that the other people of America first noticed our music, and that ours was different from theirs. Theirs was the age of jazz, of Bessie Smith and Louis Armstrong. When radio began to take an interest in us, it little realized that our music would have such an impact on the world. Needless to say, it certainly did not realize the impact which this music would have on radio itself.

On March 16, 1922, WSB in Atlanta reportedly became the first radio station to feature country music and thus began a movement that would offer our southern folk singers an opportunity to perform and give most of us an opportunity to listen to the music we loved.

Rapidly the barn dances became centers of attention—the National Barn Dance, WLS, Chicago, 1924; WSM Barn Dance, Nashville, 1925; WWVA Jamboree, Wheeling, 1926; and then the Midwestern Hayride and Renfro Valley, WLW, Cincinnati, 1937. These grew to such popularity that many of our singers grew into esteemed commercial performers, and our music was carried around the world.

Although some of the barn dances continued for years, it gradually became obvious that WSM's, the Grand Ole Opry, was establishing itself as the reigning queen of such programs—all others were becoming her subjects. This Grand Ole Lady was largely responsible for the impact which country music had on radio. And her performers were her ambassadors. Through WSM's Saturday night program, they became known all over America, and wherever Americans went. During World War II, a two-week popularity contest held on the Armed Forces Network's "Munich Morning Report" gave Roy Acuff, out of 3,700 votes cast, a lead of 600 votes over popular crooner Frank Sinatra. And in 1947, a unit of the Grand Ole Opry, headed by Ernest Tubb, became the first country group to be featured in concert at Carnegie Hall in New York City.

The influence of the Opry and other barn dance programs, especially that of WLS in Chicago, was so powerful that by 1943 the Special Services Division of the European Theatre of Operations included at least twenty-five hillbilly bands. By 1949, at least 650 radio stations used live hillbilly talent, and by 1961 country music accounted for over 30 percent of the programming of the Armed Forces Network.

As the Opry grew, its listening audience grew . . . to the point that today an estimated 35 million people around the world hear the program. Because of the Opry's popularity, the steady flow of country music has increased on radio. Over 3,000 radio stations in the United States and Canada now program at least some country music every day, 1,116 have at least two hours of such every day, and over 1,000 stations schedule country music exclusively. In other words, one out of every three radio stations is broadcasting country music some time during the day while one out of every eight broadcasts it exclusively. There was no way for WSM, in 1925, to realize that its fledgling would have such an impact on radio.

Although it was through radio that the Grand Ole Opry first became widely known, phonograph records made it a thriving business and its stars famous. Although Ralph Peer of Okeh Records came to Atlanta in 1923 and recorded Fiddlin' John Carson, and Al Hopkins and his "hillbillies" from North Carolina and Virginia had been recorded in New York in January of 1925, the recording industry had paid very little attention to our music before the late 1920s. But in August, 1927, when Peer came to Bristol, Tennessee, in search of talent, a door was opened in that industry that has never closed. He recorded the Carter Family, A. P., Sara, and Maybelle, singing *Bury Me Under the Weeping Willow,* and the next day he recorded Jimmie Rodgers in the same room. The knot which bound this industry to our music was tied when these became the first commercially successful recordings of country music. We are proud that we helped strengthen this bond by saving our hard-earned money to buy copies of these first records.

Our music had scarcely been recognized before the stock market crash of 1929. But that incident made the recording industry realize what a powerful hold country music had on the lives of its listeners; hillbilly records continued to sell steadily during the Depression, while other record sales declined markedly. Many of us who lacked the money to buy not only luxuries but necessities still spent a portion of our scant incomes on these records sung by others like us who knew poverty but who encouraged us to "keep on the sunny side." Even at the most critical points of shellac rationing during World War II, the companies continued without interruption to release hillbilly records because we continued to buy them. And our songs were longlived! Montgomery Ward and Sears catalogues carried our favorite records year after year. Bradley Kincaid's *Fatal Wedding* was listed in the Sears catalogue from 1929 to 1940.

It was not until the mid-1940s that the recording industry actually recognized its gold mine in Nashville. Prior to this time, the Grand Ole Opry stars had been going to New York to record, but the overwhelming number of country music records being sold forced the producers to change the pattern. In 1945, Paul Cohen of Decca recorded Red Foley in WSM's Studio B and the die was cast. Then George Reynolds, Aaron Shelton, and Carl Jenkins opened the "Castle Studio" in the Tulane Hotel, and Nashville was on its way to becoming a recording center.

Other companies began producing their country music material in Nashville because so much of the talent was already there . . . at the Grand Ole Opry. The Opry's impact on worldwide record business was becoming very obvious.

Then came proof positive of country music's prosperity. Pee Wee King's *Tennessee Waltz* was recorded by pop singer Patti Page in November, 1950; by December it was the nation's favorite, and by May, 1951, it had sold 4.8 million records and grossed for its writers and publishers $330,000. This song, which became the biggest hit in modern popular music history, introduced hillbilly music into the pop field and gave it a major place in the recording business. And its roots were at the Grand Ole Opry!

It was actually through records that our music had the greatest international impact. In Canada, the Toronto metropolitan area is home to over 200 country music clubs, and its Locarno Ballroom is described as a small Grand Ole Opry. Because of the influence of American military personnel, country music is at home in Europe. In 1968, families in the United States Armed Forces in Europe bought $7 million worth of records at base PX's; 65 percent of them were country and western, and at one time the percentage reached as high as 72 percent.

Our music is so well-liked in England that there is a British Country

Music Association which publishes a journal filled with advertisements promoting the annual International Festival of Country Music, featuring such Opry stars as Loretta Lynn, Conway Twitty, Bill Anderson, and George Hamilton IV. It also encourages the English to visit the Nashville Room, located in West Kensington, London, and to go to Nashville by charter flights—"Nashville Trip to Fan Fair."

On one afternoon in 1971, Tokyo's Hibiya Park was alive for seven hours with a Bluegrass Festival, giving the Japanese another opportunity to hear our music, in addition to their regularly televised "Tokyo Grand Ole Opry" and their often-chartered planes from Tokyo to Nashville to visit our Opry.

Sweden has a Country Music Association, which publishes regular bulletins using the slogan "Happiness is Country Music." Because of the influence of soldiers whom she met during the war, Kitty Prins of Antwerp has developed in Belgium the most popular country and western radio show in Europe. Switzerland now has a "Hillbilly Magazine" and a regular country music radio station. Germany has a Texas store where country music and cowboy costumes can be bought, and there are three Dutch radio shows devoted exclusively to country music.

Australia, which has a regular Country Music Awards program, produced the world's foremost expert on country music in John Edwards, who spent his life studying various aspects of American culture. He documented this study with commercial phonograph records of folk music from the period 1923–41. In his will he stated that he wanted this material to be used for furtherance of scholarly interest. Thus the John Edwards Memorial Foundation was established at the University of California at Los Angeles to house this Australian's collection.

And the root of this international interest in country music records is none but our Grand Ole Opry. This radio program was the original source from which Nashville built a recording empire, an empire which now produces 52 percent of America's records from its forty resident recording producers, forty-two recording studios, and six pressing plants.

When we first started visiting WSM's Studio A, our music was simple and steeped in folk tradition—songs that had been handed down for generations. But during the years that the Grand Ole Opry grew, it gave birth to many new ideas in song and instrumentation. Over the airwaves of WSM, novel concepts were projected; some were original with performers . . . some were merely concepts which had influenced them.

Although the Opry was not fortunate enough to present the original Carter Family, it has projected the family's influence through many performers and, of course, through one of the original group, Maybelle Carter. Bud Wendell, general manager of the Opry, has stated that "their influence is so strong it cannot be measured. Whether they know it or not, every country music person owes something to the Carter family." Although all of us who bought records during the Depression will never forget the harmony of the group or the songs A. P. Carter wrote, the thing we remember most is the guitar-playing style of Maybelle (now she is known as Mother Maybelle, but many of us remember her from earlier days).

After 1927, all of us who attempted to play an instrument considered it the height of accomplishment to learn the Maybelle Carter guitar style, and if we could copy her rendition of *Wildwood Flower,* we were prouder than if we had stripped a half-acre of tobacco before dinner time. We have been told that if you listen to her technique you can begin to understand where the Nashville Sound originated. She had learned to play a style called "drop thumb" banjo when she was a little girl, and she continued using a thumb pick when she took up the guitar. She would pick the melody on the bass strings with her thumb, an unusual style that was new to us, and at the same time play rhythm on the high strings with her fingers. We have listened in awe while she played the autoharp, an instrument for which she is equally noted, but her greatest influence on modern music is through her style in guitar picking. We owe much to this woman who has been called the "Queen Mother of Country Music" and "one of the most imitated of guitar players."

The guitar, fiddle, banjo, and mandolin have always been favorites of ours. Therefore, Bill Monroe, Lester Flatt, and Earl Scruggs are very big names to us. It was the music they created that we loved; it didn't matter what it was called. The sound usually associated with Bill Monroe became known to everyone as "bluegrass" because his string band was the Blue Grass Boys. This sound, described by Monroe as a combination of church music, jazz, and mountain fiddling, was at its peak from 1945 to 1948. Almost every Saturday night we listened as the Grand Ole Opry presented Bill Monroe with his mandolin as the lead instrument, Earl Scruggs with his five-string banjo, Lester Flatt singing the lead, Chubby Wise on the fiddle, and Cedric Rainwater on the bass playing such favorites of ours as *Will You be Lovin' Another Man* and *Blue Yodel #4.*

In 1948, Flatt and Scruggs formed the Foggy Mountain Boys, became known as the best bluegrass group in the nation, and sold enough bags of flour to make Martha White Mills an established firm. Americans who had never cared for our music found something appealing in bluegrass. Soon it was heard everywhere, and both Bill Monroe and Earl Scruggs became synonymous with it. Monroe, now billed as "The Father of Bluegrass," penned 250–300 songs, including *Blue Moon of Kentucky* which was the first song recorded by Elvis Presley when he started an entirely new style of music. Although it never would have occurred to us in 1939 when we saw Monroe for the first time on the Opry, his influence on music in America became very powerful . . . so powerful that on November 12, 1973, he appeared in an afternoon workshop in the Smithsonian's Hall of Fame of Musical Instruments and at an evening workshop in the Museum of Natural History to standing-room-only.

Those of us who like the banjo owe as much to Earl Scruggs as those who favor the guitar owe to Maybelle Carter. At a time when the five-string banjo was becoming almost obsolete, Scruggs developed a three-finger technique so that the banjo could lead as well as play background. By the time he joined Bill Monroe in 1945, he had perfected this technique which had become known as the "Scruggs style." Today we all consider Earl Scruggs the world's greatest banjo player, and we aren't alone in our opinion. One music critic has stated that "Earl Scruggs, at half pace, is the best five-string banjo picker in the world." Scruggs has written a book, *Earl Scruggs and the Five-String Banjo,* that many of us have studied and used. He and Dr. Nat Winston did "Folk Music in Tennessee," a segment of educational television's film series on the history of Tennessee, and in 1971, we all watched the Public Broadcasting System's 90-minute special called "Earl Scruggs: His Family and Friends," which featured guests Joan Baez and Bob Dylan. We are proud of the impact which these people have made on the world . . . from the stage of the Grand Ole Opry.

We have watched as many of the newer people on the Opry have influenced international music trends. We listened to the Everly Brothers sing *Bye, Bye Love,* and although it wasn't what we had been accustomed to, we bought many of their 35 million records. And we were proud when we read in the papers about their popularity in Britain where a new group called the Beatles were referring to themselves as the "English Everly Brothers" because they had been influenced so much by the harmony style of these two. And we read with special pride about how our friends on the Opry have gradually changed America's taste to accept our music more and more.

The upsurge of the fiddling we love so much has taken America by storm—Deer Creek Fiddlers Convention, north of Baltimore; Banjo and Fiddle Contest in Los Angeles; Darrington Tar Heel Day in Everett, Washington; Montana State Fiddlers Contest; Ice Cream Social and Fun Day in Parkersburg, West Virginia; Fiddler's Picnic in Rochester, New York, and many others are attracting thousands of people. America's tastes have changed from a time when our music of straightforward talk, sprinkled with the "ain'ts" of our speech pattern, was totally ignored by anyone outside the rural South to a time when the "Shindig at Cripple Creek" held outside Lancaster, Pennsylvania, during the summer of 1974 featured Tanya Tucker, Mel Tillis, the Chuck Wagon Gang with Jimmie Davis, Rick Nelson, the Osborne Brothers, the Stoney Mountain Cloggers, Merle Haggard, Bill Anderson, George Jones and Tammy Wynette, Buck Owens, Lynn Anderson, and the Oak Ridge Boys. Quite a schedule for an area outside the rural South!

The Grand Ole Opry has touched all America, but its effect on the city of its birth has been of particular interest to us. We have seen the music industry, which has sprung from the Opry, virtually make Nashville into what it now is. The music industry is reportedly worth $250 million annually to Nashville, and although there is no way we can imagine such a sum of money, we can see its impact in the buildings we pass and the activity they represent. It is obvious that the music industry looms high over any other endeavor in this city of almost one-half million people.

We made music that was different . . .

As the Opry became more popular, many from the top-ranking country talent began to make their homes in or near Nashville. As the singers moved in, so did the music business—the booking agents, the artists and repertoire men, the promoters. By the late 1930s, WSM's Artists Bureau, directed by James Denny, had become a big business and was sending the stars to tour many of our communities. Gradually such outside promoters as Joe Frank, Oscar Davis, and Colonel Tom Parker (whom almost everyone knows as Elvis Presley's manager) began to take part in the scene, and the promotion business grew. Wherever they sent the Opry stars, we went to see them. In 1956, Denny left WSM and established his own bureau, and in 1961 he alone handled over 3,200 personal appearances throughout the world. Today there are over 100 talent agents, booking agencies, or personal managers located in Nashville and handling a touring system that allows 7 to 8 million of us to see the Opry stars in our own hometowns and communities.

When Roy Acuff teamed with Wesley Rose and formed Acuff–Rose Publications in 1943, he did so because there were so many songwriters working in Nashville. Today over 900 of them call Nashville home and, as a result, over 400 music publishers either have home offices in Nashville or are represented by an office there.

After Decca began recording its country music talent in Nashville, most major companies followed suit and, together, they built a recording center. Although we don't see most of this activity, there are over 15,000 recording sessions a year in Nashville. In order for this to take place, every type of business connected with the recording industry is now represented there. There are over 300 record labels located in the city, over 55 recording studios, one shipping service which exclusively serves the music trade, 9 public relations and promotion agencies for the music business, 6 pressing and plating plants, 5 record distributors, 2 rack jobbers; 13 design and artwork firms serving the industry, 5 direct mail firms, 4 tape duplication companies, 13 still photography firms dealing almost exclusively with music, and over 50 artists and repertoire (A&R) men. We can see these statistics change almost daily as new companies take over old buildings or construct new ones in Nashville.

All the businesses connected with the recording industry would wither and die without the talent for which they operate. By the late 1950s, the musicians residing in Nashville could rival in proficiency and skill musicians from anywhere else in the United States. They played together so much that they knew each other's styles and the styles of the country singers for whom they played. With the building of the recording industry, their skills were in great demand. Today Nashville's local chapter of the American Federation of Musicians (Local #257) has over 1,700 members, and the American Federation of Television and Radio Artists' local chapter has between 600 and 700 members.

When we drive through the streets of Nashville and its outlying towns we find that some of the most unusual and beautiful homes belong to the country music stars. From the north of the city, where Johnny Cash's $250,000 home spreads along the bank of Old Hickory Lake, to the south of Nashville, where the estates of Webb Pierce and Minnie Pearl are separated by the Governor's Mansion, we are able to see how the Opry has affected Nashville.

Country music owes much of its success to Broadcast Music, Incorporated which, when founded in 1939, offered a great opportunity to country music composers. Formed as a strike against the American Society of Composers, Authors, and Publishers, which allegedly had almost totally ignored country songwriters, it readily accepted these writers. During the first ten months of 1941, BMI expanded a catalogue to over 36,000 copyrights from 52 publishers, many of which were country. From that time on, the country music songwriter was able to get proper licensing for his work. Now there are 3 licensing and performing rights societies in Nashville as well as 12 associations and professional organizations dealing with music.

Because television has allowed many of us to get a good view of the stars without going to the Opry, Nashville is now the home of 8 syndication firms, turning out such programs as "The Bill Anderson Show" (syndicated to over 110 stations), "Good Ole Nashville Music," "The Wilburn Brothers," and "The Porter Wagoner Show" (seen by 4,471,000 viewers on over 100 syndicated stations). The success of such programs moved *Variety* to comment that "the real winner of the Nielsen market-by-market November '72 syndication sweeps is the city of Nashville." These shows are primarily responsible for the fact that half the nation's television stations program some gospel or country shows. Other businesses, such as 11 motion picture firms and 7 jingle and commercial spot firms, have moved into Nashville because of fertile advantages sown by the music industry.

We see that the music industry provides much of Nashville's life blood; and although this industry through its growth has encompassed many other businesses, it owes its existence to the Grand Ole Opry. The Opry is not only indirectly responsible for the entire music industry of Nashville, it also directly contributes to Nashville's economy by attracting some 750,000 of us each year who would not be going there if it were not to see the Grand Ole Opry. We bring Nashville tremendous tourist business. We come from everywhere to stay a few days, spend an average of $50 per person a day, and then go home to tell everyone that he must go and see it too. Statistics confirm that in the average weekly audience at the Opry there are *at least* four of us from each state in the Union except Nevada —and there's one from Nevada. In the average audience, there are six from Japan, four from Ireland, two each from Holland, Belgium, Germany, England, Australia, and Vietnam, and one from Denmark and from Hawaii. That represents a lot of people in Nashville on the same day!

The recent construction of the 369-acre amusement park called Opryland, U.S.A. is perhaps the Opry's biggest impact on the city of Nashville to date. This $28 million complex opened in 1972 and produced revenues of

$14.3 million the following year. In addition to housing many rides, restaurants, and the New Grand Ole Opry House, Opryland gives 1,700 teenagers summer employment and brings to Nashville 1.7 million visitors annually. These visitors obviously need accommodations. Consequently, although 8,000 motel rooms were already available in a 20-mile radius of the city, 1,500 more rooms were added in 1973 and 1,868 more in 1974.

The effect the Opry has had on Nashville could never be overstated. Its direct impact through its own performances, tours of the city, and Opryland can hardly be estimated in terms of money. Its indirect impact through the music industry, apart from the Opry, is estimated conservatively at a quarter of a billion dollars annually. Perhaps its impact can best be felt by realizing that a corner lot on 17th Avenue (part of Music Row) sold for $39,000 in January, 1965, and the buyer refused $160,000 for it the following January, and that a 50-foot lot could be bought for $15,000 in 1961 but was priced at $80,000 five years later. The visitor to Music Row a few years ago saw a dilapidated house opposite the Country Music Hall of Fame; now he sees Nashville's 42-suite, luxury Spence Manor Motor Hotel, where every suite has its own dining area, and each guest is served his meals in private by room service. Strictly first class!

Nashville is thriving from the music industry and its byproducts. But as it continues to grow and prosper, the city never forgets its debt to the Grand Ole Lady who started it all—the Grand Ole Opry.

The Grand Ole Lady has had tremendous impact:

On radio . . .

The Wilburn Brothers

On the recording industry . . .

Johnny Cash

Tree Recording Company

Broadcast Music, Incorporated

On television . . .

Loretta Lynn and Minnie Pearl on Mike Douglas Show

Minnie with Dinah

Marty Robbins and Wolfman Jack on TV special

Johnny Cash and Minnie Pearl

On the music industry . . .

Chet Atkins, the most influential man in Music City.

She has had influence on unique musical styles . . .

Bill Monroe and his "bluegrass"

Mother Maybelle Carter, "Queen Mother of Country Music," who developed a unique "drop thumb" method of picking a banjo or guitar.

Earl Scruggs, "the world's greatest banjo player," with Lester Flatt.

On individual performers outside the Opry . . .

Charlie Pride

Jeannie C. Riley

The Silver Fox, Charlie Rich

On people who never dreamed they could be stars.

Jan Howard, a waitress and "hunt and peck" secretary until stardom.

National Life and Accident Insurance Company Building

State Capitol complex surrounded by growing city

Country Music Hall of Fame

Opryland

Minnie Pearl with Winfield Dunn, her next door neighbor while Governor.

Tremendous impact on the State of Tennessee and region . . .

In 1947, an Opry unit, headed by Ernest Tubb,
became the first country group to be featured at Carnegie Hall.

Flatt & Scruggs on Grand Ole Opry inaugural float in Washington, D.C.

Impact on the world.

Tokyo Grand Ole Opry

Hank Snow

George Hamilton IV and Loretta Lynn
at International Festival of Country Music in London.

Minnie Pearl on Tom Jones Show

ACKNOWLEDGMENT

Grateful acknowledgment is made to Mrs. Tex Ritter, who as Director of Entertainment Industry Relations, Department of Economic and Community Development, of the State of Tennessee, provided invaluable assistance in arranging appointments with personalities of the Grand Ole Opry.

PHOTO CREDITS

Country Music Foundation Library and Media Center, Nashville, Tennessee—8, 21, 22, 26, 32, 33, 46, 57, 60–62, 80–85, 87, 98, 100 (bottom left), 103 (bottom), 104, 109–10, 111 (top), back of jacket.

Tennessee Tourism Development—23, 25, 27, 29–31, 34–36, 43–45, 47–49, 107 (top right; bottom left).

Cookeville *Herald–Citizen*—24

Nashville *Banner*—6, 51 (top), 63, 86, 99 (top), 100 (top left; top right; bottom right), 108, 111 (bottom).

Myron Tassin—14, 53, 55, 65, 68, 72, 102, 106, front of jacket (center).

Jerry Henderson—28

Columbus *Dispatch*—51 (bottom).

Bill MacMillan—99 (bottom left; bottom right).

Baton Rouge *Sunday Advocate*—101, 105.

Public Library of Nashville and Davidson County, Naff Collection—50, 52, 54, 56, 59, 107 (top left).

Bud Lee—66–67.

Marshall Folwell, Jr.—front of jacket (left center).

Gordon H. Schenck, Jr.—70–71, 107 (bottom right), front of jacket (bottom).

Causey Photography—69, front of jacket (right center).

Maybelle Carter—10, 103 (top).